Anthony L. Oliver

The Book
of
OLIVER

Motivational Awakenings
To Live a More Productive Life....

The Book of Oliver: Motivational Awakenings to Live a More Purposeful Life

Published and Distributed by Anthony L. Oliver, Norwalk, Connecticut

Book Coach – Robin Devonish
Cover Design – Okomota
Editing – Pen Publish Profit, LLC
Interior Design – www.queekpub.com

ISBN: 979-8-9875547-0-8

Printed in the United States of America

ACKNOWLEDGEMENTS

I began this journey because I wanted to be called an author. Since then, my reasons have drastically changed. I discovered there's a gift inside of me that must be shared with the world.

First, I thank my awesome wife Jocelyn who has been with me every step of the way.

Next, I thank my two sons Christian and Austin, who were born during the process.

I thank any future child that God may bless us with.

I thank Triumphant Christian Church, under the tutelage of my pastor Apostle Cynthia G. West. Due to the many relationships and conversations, I've had with my fellow believers, I was able to come up with a lot of what's in this book.

DEDICATION

This book is dedicated to keeping the name 'Oliver' alive.

This book plants the seed for many great things to happen.

I thank my mother and father Bessie and George Oliver.

I thank my sisters Lashonda and Andrea Oliver

I thank my brother George Oliver.

I thank Dikyree Oliver.

I'm fortunate for the knowledge given to me from my parents in love, Mrs. Cynthia, and Mr. Arthur West.

Special acknowledgements to the Williams, Gee, West and Oliver families. You all have a special place in my life.

Shout out to Kwame and the 7th and 8th grade Sheehan Cardinal Basketball teams who encouraged me to finish this book.

Thanks to everyone that supported this project.

A LITTLE ABOUT ME...

I was born and raised in Norwalk Connecticut. For the most part, it was a great place to grow up. Living there taught me a lot while sitting in the park and watching life happen. Every so often you'd hear gunshots, or a fight break out at the local bar. I was a good kid in school but very mischievous. I would never get into trouble while in class, so the teachers wouldn't think or know of that 'sweet innocent Anthony could never do anything wrong'.

My parents George and Bessie worked hard daily to support our family. Watching them was where I learned my work ethics.

I looked up to both my sisters because they were very smart. My brother and I got along very well.

My two biggest vices were basketball and video games. I was a quiet kid with two personas. I was Anthony in school, the perfect student that every teacher would love to have in their classroom. At home I was Tony, the fun loving very chill guy. The older I got, the less I liked to talk. The only time I talked was on the basketball court and it became a place where I learned my toughness. Being a non-talker for many years, I was able to pick up more by listening.

I met my wife in my mid-twenties, and she challenged me to be more. I wouldn't have my masters' degree today and on my way to my doctorate if it wasn't for her. As we were in the courting process, she introduced me to her church. I fell in love with the ministry and began to serve each Sunday. While serving, fellow members would always pull me to the side and share wisdom with me. I started learning about topics like forgiveness and love from the preaching I heard over the pulpit each week.

Being in a new atmosphere led me to start reading and watching motivational videos. And, once I went back to college, before I knew it I was full of this special knowledge that I had to share with the world.

CONTENTS

GOD

Some people work so hard at being important, that they miss out on the importance of why we are put on this Earth.

• • •

It seems that everyone wants to be a star. However, some of the greatest things happen in the backroom. Some of the most famous people had to work in the back before becoming the headliner. Pursuing 'stardom' can cause you to get off track. Take a safe and legal u-turn and find out what God's purpose is for your life.

Sometimes you must lend someone your faith.

• • •

When you're not connected to the right power source, your energy can become low. In a world surrounded by negativity, doubt and under-utilization of your gifts, you can get lost. Like WIFI, you must get connected to a "hotspot" and get charged up. Once you're charged up, lend someone else your charger through your testimony, experiences and wisdom.

One of the biggest issues is that many people think that their life is their own.

• • •

The more you try to do for yourself, the less you will have. The more you do for others, the more you will have. Having a 'me first' mentality isn't a horrible thing; it's just the wrong way of thinking. We are put on this earth to be an answer to a problem. Finding the problem is what your life's journey is about. We can't just live life the way we want to. Life is always bigger than us.

Aspiring not to be great is also a sin.

• • •

We are all put on this earth to do great and powerful things. Many never reach their potential because they don't believe in themselves. There is a great power in you yearning to come out. Every moment that you're not pushing to greatness, is a moment that you're rejecting the true purpose of why God has you here on this Earth.

You can't beat a system that is designed to bring you down. If you are trying to beat a system, you're operating out of the wrong one.

•••

The systems of this world are just that, systems. You should be connected to a greater power source. Once you shift your lens to see clearer, you will realize the battle is not physical but spiritual. Once realized, this is the point where things begin to change.

Every blessing has a cost, don't short change it.

• • •

Blessings are really tests to see how you will handle them. There's also a price you must pay. Never let blessings surprise you but be prepared for the consequences.

Hope is a never-ending journey.

• • •

Hope fuels your faith! There are people that have everything they need but still aren't happy. No matter what level you're on in life, you must have something to reach for. Without it, you will lose your sense of existence.

A title doesn't mean anything unless you answer to
a higher power.

• • •

No matter how far you go in this world, you must answer
to a higher calling. For even a man without faith will have to
answer to someone or something. Many powerful people
come together to pray and seek wisdom. They asked NASA
what they do when a meteor is headed toward the earth
and they said, "We pray."

You have to let people go out and be great and they will come back and share the good news.

• • •

Lebron James was so hated for leaving Cleveland that they burned his jersey at the stake. Does that sound familiar? Once he learned how to win, he came back and brought the city a championship.

It takes a certain level of submission to make it in specific arenas.

• • •

Some of the most successful people set intentional time to pray each week. Even though they don't have a boss in the natural world, they seek guidance and understanding from a higher power. Most don't make it to the level of success they should because they are not committed to the submission.

A true believer fills in where there's a need.

• • •

Fill in whatever gap in this world that is needed. I may not know how to cook well, but I can also wash a dish or sweep the floor. The more you serve the higher you go.

Your praise is your qualification.

• • •

One thing God does not do is worship himself. Too many people take credit for what God did. Even the non-believer gives credit where credit is due. Give God his due credit and more will come. Be selfish and ungrateful and watch the well dry up.

WISDOM

My beautiful wife once told me this and it makes so much sense now.

• • •

"The man has the vision, but the woman is the glasses to make sight clearer." -Jocelyn Oliver

You will go further, once you know how the game is played. Find who you are in the game, learn the rules and use them to your advantage.

• • •

Life is nothing but a game. "You have to know who the key players are and who's on your side." -Apostle Cynthia G. West

At some point in life, you must put stupid down and grow up.

• • •

When we were young, we thought like children and did childish things. The problem is many of us have brought this type of thinking into our adult lives. Life is not reality wrapped up the way we want it. You will need to compromise. The curve ball never stops coming, so be prepared to not be prepared.

There's no such thing as a convenient sacrifice.

• • •

Sacrifices are hard, people go out of their way to help others and complain about what they receive in return. Sacrifices have two requirements. You first must give something up. The second is not to always expect something in return. Don't dwell on what you lost, but be grateful for the lesson you learned.

People who never make it usually spends the day reflecting on how they never made it. Where is the mind shift?

•••

Refuse to stand on the sideline watching other people live successful lives. You have a divine reason for being on this Earth. Everyone has talents, gifts and opportunities. Once you prepare for those roads to cross, you will not only be successful, but success becomes who you are.

The worst thing you can do is to go into business to make money. What is your reasonable service to this world?

• • •

A vast majority of individuals who go into business just to make money fail. You have to find out what service you can give this world and do it with a passion. As you change the world, the finances will come. The "pursuit" of money is the root of all evil because it can drive people to do ungodly things.

Knowledge can be passed through a whisper or a sound.

• • •

Everything in life is a learning experience, and many times, not loud. It's not a motivational speech; it could just be a calm sound. Use every opportunity to learn and grow from not only the loud, but the quiet.

Sometimes life comes at you so fast that you must purposely slow down just to live it. Look to the future but stop and understand the now.

• • •

The most successful athletes are able to slow the game down. They can assess the situation and think one step ahead of their opponent. Don't be afraid to change your plan mid-game.

You're being dishonest with the world when you don't leave anything behind.

• • •

It's a privilege to be on this Earth. Don't take for granted the opportunity you have to make it better. As the old Blockbuster saying goes, "be kind and rewind". Anything you are given, make sure it's returned in a better state than found.

Just because you support a situation, doesn't make it right.

• • •

A situation may feel right in your heart, but it doesn't make it right with the creator. We all make decisions in moments of split seconds, just to rectify a situation. Strategically you should assess every situation because there are always ramifications.

Your title doesn't qualify you for a position.

• • •

You can get a title because you are good friends with somebody. When you prepare for success, the opportunity will make room for you. Study to show yourself approved.

Hitting a goal means you must keep going.

• • •

Success can become a distraction in life. Success, can also become the biggest cause for failure. If you look at the greatest athletes, they never celebrate for a long period of time. Michael Jordan got upset at his Hall of Fame speech because he felt like he reached his apex. Always strive to do more, even if it's not for you and yours. Do it for generations to come.

Laziness is one of the biggest killers of dreams.

• • •

Laziness is like a sickness that takes over your mind and body. Flip the script, give it all you have for three consecutive months and see what happens.

People say 'Chivalry' is dead. However, it goes beyond opening doors and pulling out chairs. It's standing up for a set of beliefs and not wavering from your standard.

• • •

Chivalry doesn't change depending on who's around you. A standard is never broken unless it's not really a standard at all.

Average = Comfortable

• • •

The average person goes through the same daily routine. Get up, go to work, go home, and eat dinner. The people that get tired of the status quo are those that stand up and make a change. All it takes is something inside you to snap to realize that 'average' isn't for me. You are one snap away from greatness.

ENCOUR

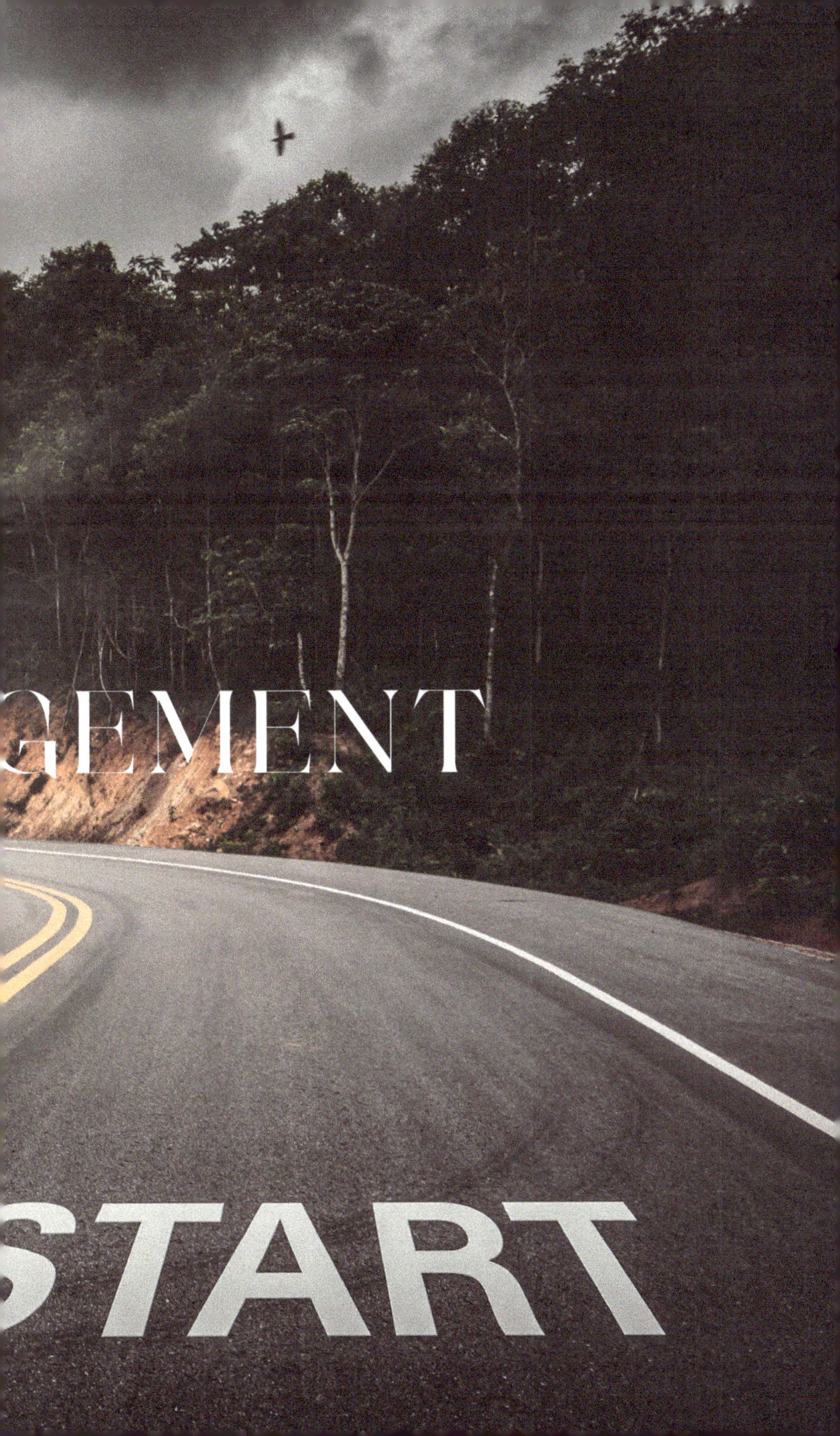
GEMENT
START

Comfortability is settling at subpar living. Push past the norm to discover your destiny.

• • •

Every person can become a changed person. Look at yourself daily and think how you can become a better person. Always look to the positive and stay away from temptation. Hold the ones you love close and keep God first. Change your life, become more purposeful in your thinking.

You don't have to chase success, just stay on the
right path and it will find you.

• • •

There's a saying, "get up, dress up, and show up." Embrace
this mindset in your daily life. Find a mirror and look at
yourself. You're looking into the soul of greatness. Your
purpose in life may just be to prepare yourself for this very
moment.

Just because you're not where you want to be, doesn't make you a failure. It just means that success is on the horizon.

• • •

It took me five years to achieve a two year degree. Then after taking nearly ten years off, I retired from working to obtain my bachelor's degree. I completed my master's degree shortly after. I thought I was done for good but now I'm hard at work to obtain my doctorate. Take your timeline and toss it out the window and find out what your appointed time is.

Some battles you win by just showing up.

• • •

When you really understand how the world works, some battles won't capture your attention. The victory has already been spoken in your life. Sometimes you have to prepare for the victory, even before the battle.

A job can't stop your greatness.

• • •

I remember sitting at my 9 to 5 dreaming about how I was going to get my business off the ground. Even though they saw me as a quiet, well-behaved employee, I was so much more. If your current situation limits you, it's time to move on. Every move on the board should be towards your endgame.

You don't need a million jobs to make a million dollars. Eliminate the poverty mindset.

• • •

When you find your rhythm and purpose, you can easily make money with little effort. Not having enough is the poverty mindset. Once you realize you have everything you need for life, you become unstoppable.

There's no need to chase success, just keep doing what you should and success will find you.

• • •

Either you have what it takes to be successful or you're failing to acknowledge that you do.

The only thing stopping you is you. Make it happen!

• • •

You should be your biggest critic. If you did a good job, you can always do better. 100% is not enough and compliments don't mean anything.

Before you believed in yourself, someone else
believed in you.

• • •

Someone is always sitting on the sideline watching you.
They may never say a word to you, but they knew you had
potential.

A step for betterment is a step in the right
direction.

• • •

Everyone goes through struggle, regret and sadness in their
life. All it takes is one good thought and you're out. If you
lost your job, then go get a better one. If your significant
other left you, take something positive out of the situation.
The only way to go is up, unless you prefer to go in the
other direction.

Sometimes God start's you over from scratch, just to see how you will build yourself back up.

• • •

Sometimes, you lose everything in life, but for a good reason. God wants to see how you will use your faith to recover. Some choose to take the easier route of stealing and cheating to regain what was lost. The test isn't if you will come back, but how! Make sure you come out the fire not smelling like you were in it.

Don't filter out your true beauty.

• • •

There's nothing more beautiful than something in its natural state. This is the form that it's truly meant to be in. Many times we put "filters" on things and think they will look better. True beauty was there all along. You just weren't seeing properly.

The one missing ingredient for your success is trying.

• • •

Stop letting life beat you up, let alone people. Get up and respond, let the elements know who you are.

Sometimes you have to start out as the dishwasher
before you can own the restaurant.

• • •

Learn every aspect of a job and stay a servant no matter how
high you go. The more you serve, the greater you become.
After all, the servant knows more about the house than the
owner.

Your failures make you the person you are today.

• • •

Sometimes failure is a gift. You can come out of the storm thinking, 'what is my reward?' Your reward is in what you experienced. Then you can take your knowledge and use it to help someone else. Your reward comes when you are not seeking it.

LOVE

Some people don't love you as much as they could because you won't give them the chance.

• • •

Forgiveness is one of the most powerful words in this world. Many know it, but lack of it hinders greatness. The person that hurt you in the past might not be the same person you dislike today. We've seen a lot of strange things happen in this post pandemic world. Don't miss an opportunity to love on someone.

You are no better than people, but sometimes you are the positive change they are missing in their lives.

• • •

We are meant to be the little bit of light in someone's life that makes a difference. When the light shines, darkness is eliminated.

Your heart may be in it, but your head is not.

• • •

A simple tug of the heart can get you emotionally involved. If your thoughts are not healthy, then you can easily get pulled by a stray.

OUGHTS

You are what you eat! So, what you feed your
mind determines your thought process.

•••

One day, I was reading and discovered that when you change
the way you think, your body becomes conditioned to the
new thought process. The more violence and doubt you
feed your mind with, your body prepares for it. The more
you enhance, challenge and stretch your mind, the greater
capacity you will have. Positivity and knowledge go a long
way.

> If you are succeeding on a losing team, then what
> does that say about the success?

• • •

You probably heard the saying a million times; the people around you make a major difference. You must know the players on your team, who you can trust, who's out for personal gain, and who has your best interest. If they are not enhancing you, then trade them to another team. If you're not enhancing them, why are they on your team?

We always take credit when we accomplish something, but it's someone else's fault when we fail. The equation is unbalanced.

• • •

Own up to the mistakes you make. No matter how far you go in life, always remember those who helped you get there. Be ready to reach down to pull someone up. Success should be shared!

Your biggest opponent is yourself!

• • •

The man in the mirror is a true concept. The biggest challenge is within self. Stop trying to be the best version of someone else. Once you realize that you can do all things and there's a great power inside of you; the journey will truly start. You have to ignite the fire inside of you and work like your life depended on it.

Don't get caught in the prison of your own mind.

• • •

When a person gets stuck in all the victories they didn't win, they then become a prisoner in their mind. Having your thoughts stuck in one place distracts you from where you are going. Take all wasted energy and redirect it to your next victory. Take the broken record off the track and begin to dance to a new tune.

Free your mind from the captivity of this world.

• • •

The mind is very fragile. Tipped the wrong way, it can go off kilter. If given the right information, the mind can expand and grow. A new perspective goes a mighty long way.

REMINDERS

Some people naturally aren't talented; they just put in the work needed to be successful.

• • •

Not everyone wants to be successful. Many people stop at a comfortable place in life. Success is not always pretty and it doesn't smell nice; achieving it requires long nights and early days. But when you cross over to the Promised Land, you will find the journey you took to get there was worth it.

Never seek an award for doing what's right, it simply is unwritten.

• • •

Sometimes we give out so much to people, but get nothing in return. This is not an indicator to stop; keep blessing, giving and seeding to others. Your blessing could just be living another day. After all, what you sow reproduces after its own kind.

Stop caring if people like you or not. That's not what life is about. It's really about how you can offer positive advancements into their lives.

• • •

The most successful person in the room is not always the loudest and the most glamorous. We live in an opinionated world. The problem is jealousy runs rampant. Even if someone tries to knock you off track, you are still obligated to help them. Remember, you are the answer to the world's problem.

Every moment we rest, we lose out on helping someone else.

• • •

Every generation deals with forces and has some issues they must struggle through. Sometimes you don't realize that the smallest gesture can turn someone else's life around. It could be a compliment, inspiration or just buying them lunch. People don't always need your advice; they need you to be present in a moment of weakness.

How dare you let people that are beneath you, get to you? These are obvious distractions.

• • •

Everyone is in your life for a purpose. In some cases, their purpose could be to get you off track. Isn't it funny that we let people who haven't achieved as much as we have get under our skin? Stay focused on your true purpose and not the comment section.

Every minute, every second, and every hour of life is important.

• • •

You must always be learning, seeking and teaching. After all, someone else might have the solution to your life. The biggest thing you can lose in life is time, because you cannot get it back.

Never judge any situation where you couldn't have done a better job.

• • •

People are quick to judge situations that they have no experience in. We have no idea what situations or pressures someone had on them to complete a task. Let's offer positive feedback instead of negative feedback.

Your life is a compilation of events that brought
you to today.

• • •

Everything happens for a reason. You must take the positive
moments and learn to make them better. Take the negative
moments and use them as ammunition. The best version of
yourself already exists; you just have to bring it out.

You can't bring everyone with you on life's journey; some people just don't have the mindset.

• • •

Everyone has a group of individuals that we think we are going to take with us when we "make it". Some don't have the capacity to breathe on the next-level. The oxygen level is too high and their morals are too low.

Before you give up an opportunity, just think about what other people would give to be in your shoes.

• • •

You've come a long way since your journey began. We all get tired along the way and our mind tricks us to think the journey wasn't worth it. Just think of all the people that would love to be in your shoes; some may even be plotting as we speak. This should be enough to motivate you and know that all the rough patches were worth it.

Don't ever think that the person you are talking to is the same person the last time you saw them. They may have moved forward.

• • •

This is a case of mistaken identity. You thought the person you went to high school with is the same person you ran into at the gas station. People can learn to grow and evolve. The Flash once told his enemy, "I got faster, didn't you"?

The person who tries to show off usually ends up looking silly.

• • •

Get out in life and meet some great people. Find out how they were able to make it. You never serve wine before its time. Great people don't usually show out, they show up. You can feel their essence in the room. Make it to the point where you can change an atmosphere just by showing up.

You can't always accept people's responses,
sometimes you have to dissect them.

• • •

People will tell you what you want to hear at that time, but
not the truth in their intentions. So, we accept things at
face value and never investigate intentions. A job may write
you up and say it's because you did something wrong, but
in reality your previous track record led to it. Know who's
running with you and who's trying to slow you down.

Never go into anything just to make money.

• • •

The love of money is the root of all evil. Money, like anything else, has a spirit. If you waste it and are not wise, it will run out. If you respect it and understand how it works, you might just obtain more.

A good support system could be the fuel your dreams need.

• • •

There will be many days where you're by yourself and don't think you can make it. This is when your support system is the most important. You need someone to say keep going, you're almost there, or you did good but you can do better. A man or a woman was never designed to do it alone.

It's impossible to fall when the right people have your back.

• • •

When you surround yourself with the right team, someone will always have your back. Even when you're at the height of success, they will push you to do more. For the jealous one in your camp may just be the Judas.

LIFE

The game of life is about how many different people's lives you can change in the course of a day.

• • •

Have you ever thought about someone in need that you could help but didn't? There are various reasons that come into play. Does this individual really need your help or are we really this selfish? You'll get a lot further in life when you realize the more you do for others, the more you will receive blessings.

In life you have to wear many hats, and you must be ready to switch them up at any time.

• • •

Now that I step back and look, I'm a Deacon, husband, father, minister, coach, mentor, brother, cousin, friend, and the list goes on. At any given time, I have to be ready to put on any of these hats. People need me and I don't have the luxury to be tired, angry or lazy. You have the knowledge inside you to change people's destiny. You must know which position you're operating in.

Struggle is a must in life. Most people don't realize success is right on the other side of the door. They take the first punch and drop out of the fight.

• • •

Mike Tyson once said, "Everyone has a strategy until you get punched in the fact." You must accept the face that failure is not part of the problem; it's an ingredient for success. Don't get so weary in the journey that you quit too early. Success isn't given to the fastest or the strongest, but the person that can endure the fight until the end.

You either leave a legacy of success or a legacy of failure.

Every decision you make is sowing a seed for your legacy. This can be something small like choosing not to dress up. The child that looks up to you may be watching. Every bad decision you make is sowing a seed in the wrong kingdom. You are either building or destroying. Choose this day who you will serve.

The problem is your lifestyle is outdated.

• • •

The American Dream once was to get a career and buy a house with a white picket fence. Now, the dream might be having a million followers on YouTube. Take time to reassess your destination, see if your lifestyle still suits where you're going.

Some of your "so called" friends might not make the cut for this next stage in life.

•••

We all had friends that did some negative things growing up. Imagine if you were still hanging around with them today. With each plateau in life, you must reexamine your circle. The higher you go, the smaller it gets. Some people's main task in life is to see you fail. Use them as steppingstones to go even higher.

You can die from living an average life.

• • •

With no purpose in life, you have no use. You must seek what's calling you. We have been made to live a life of abundance. Anything less than that is going against the plan.

Don't give all your energy to work and not enjoy life.

• • •

There will be times in your life where you have to work three to four jobs and through many sleepless nights. With the right strategies, there should come a day when you can enjoy life. I never want to make it big when it's too late for the people that paved the way to enjoy it with me.

On the journey, make sure you stop and take time to enjoy the view.

• • •

One can go through struggles, not knowing how they will end up. For once, enjoy the process and use the scenery as motivation for your next step in the journey. Your life is like a movie or a book; allow the Holy Spirit to direct and God to be your author.

Stop living life on a budget and enjoy it!

• • •

Counting your money before you get it is a poverty mindset. A wealthy man once told me that he doesn't like to take money out of the bank, so he just works harder to make more. Most work hard their whole life and have nothing to say for it. Learn the principles you need to be successful and surround yourself with people that want to live above average lives.

You can change someone's life with just a smile.

• • •

As one of my pastors would say every Sunday, "turn and give someone the gift of your smile." You have no idea what someone is going through. By taking your time and passing some positive energy, it can change the trajectory of a person's life.

You will get further in life by thinking one step further.

• • •

To win in chess, you must be one step ahead of your opponent. Sometimes revealing your next move is strategic, but in many cases strategy is silent.

Most people stop at the level of comfort.

• • •

This very book opened with a quote similar to this. When you're going up the ladder of success and then stop, that means you just straight-lined. Physically you are still alive but successfully you're dead. You may be just starting off on the path, ready too quit, even on life support; once you're ready to break that's when you fight for your life.

There's never a moment when there's not a call to action.

• • •

The choices you make in life have a cause and effect. The one time you choose not to help someone could be a test that you failed. You must seize opportunities before they expire. Don't dwell in losses too long, always keep moving forward.

There is an amazing call on your life and it's calling out to you.

• • •

To quote Thanos, one of the greatest Marvel villains said, "Run from it, dred it, destiny still arrives." We all are here for a reason. You must quiet down the movie in your head and find your purpose. It calls out to everyone but most don't answer. This is why less than 2% of people reach their fullest potential.

CLOSING

Greatness!

•••

I had a roommate that would be at my door before he left for work and say "be great." I didn't know what it meant then, but now I do. It's living the life that you are designed to so well that you glorify God and attract others.

Find something in this world that you are good at, and give it everything you got.

• • •

Every profession has a master level. If there's not one, then create the standard for it. Hard work is not enough anymore. You have to walk on the divine path.

People's biggest regret is that they didn't wait around long enough to see your greatness.

• • •

Life is like a relay race, you must be ready when the baton comes your way.

Change a mindset and you save generations.

• • •

Poverty is a mindset. Never having enough, not being enough, are all mindsets. When you change the way you look at situations, and know you have to pave the way for other; you can inspire generations to come.

It was you all the time, you were the one.

• • •

You were the one set apart to make a change the whole time and didn't know it. You were the one to bring your family out. You had the map to glory this whole time and didn't use it. I hope this book has made you realize the greatness inside of you. Take the same greatness and spread a little here and a little there.

In loving memory of my brother
George Brian Oliver
1981-2023

www.ingramcontent.com/pod-product-compliance
Lightning Source LLC
Chambersburg PA
CBHW051218120626
46547CB00013B/1404